HUES

Blue

Dedications

To the boy who burst through that front door-
thank you for running straight for me.
Your love and support are something miraculous
and you clearly have swept me off my feet.
None of this would be possible without you.

To my sweet, precious girls-
Remain honest in your pursuit and
the Light will always lead you home.
Thank you for pulling out of me a crazy
will to live a laid down life of love and authenticity.

And to every woman who has ever been told
that she can't, even if by her own self-
You can. And you will.

Authors Note

Ocean waves and clear open skies, deep night-ness and sleepy navy lullabies. Blue has always been, for me, a symbol of strength and wisdom and struggle and hurt all at once. Peaceful, sure, but complex and beautiful in every form. Hues: Blue was birthed during a time I needed to explore my own humanity and heavy emotion and often times learn to be okay with lows existing in the first place. Hues: Blue is my battle cry, my confrontation with confusion, hopelessness and hurt before living out extreme gratitude for discovery and freedom. Raise your fists with me as you thumb through every set-back, sit-down, knock-out and one more round and remember, we may feel as if we're drowning in the deepest darkest hue of blue, but we can emerge triumphant with the most beautiful turquoise heart the world has ever seen.

Stevie Saldivar

My experiences are unique, yes.
But we are all tethered by Spirit and Soul.

I'm looking through lenses, so I'll start where I reside.

-I hope this helps.

Some days I'm so sure to turn left here.
I know where to make the sharp right
and then park just over there
for two hours.

Lately, though, the fog has rolled in too thick.
I can't quite make out the next rest stop sign.

I'm headed for a tunnel and
I don't know where it will spit me out.

Stevie Saldivar

A life dedicated to:

Holiness
Faith
Good things from above
Truth
Beauty
Kindness
Empathy
Compassion
Humility
Loyalty
Standing my ground
Learning
Gentleness
Self-control
Joy
Peace
and Patience

A life dedicated to You.
A life dedicated to Love.

As I wade in darkened waters,
treading as slow as possible across an
indistinguishable murky river floor-
I know that step after step, I get a little father.

Soon, I'll look down and be able to see my own legs
and then my feet.

I'm headed for crystal clear fluidity-
The kind of water that glistens from the Son.

If I must go through this to get there, so be it.

Stevie Saldivar

I feel as if I've awoken from a dream.
The kind that sends shivers down your spine even
though you're asleep.
I was stuck running in slow motion with cement bricks
tied to my feet.

I've been remade wild
and I've been remade free.

I can reach my hand to yours if you need me dear
sister of the sky.
I can show you how I got here,
but it takes guts and it takes precious time.

If you find yourself filled with fear as I was,
take one breath or maybe two.

I'll carry you if I must-
Until you taste this sweet freedom too.

More than philosophies or rituals,
it's showing up every day while being held by the
Carrier of the stars.
Like walking hand in hand with your Beloved into
battle-
knowing no matter how bruised you may become
you will always be made stronger-
you will always see light shining into your battle scars.

Your mind is sharp and infinite-
don't be afraid to have questions.
But for the love of God,
do not let those questions shut your mouth.

I can feel my atoms reach for You.
I'm desperate for your voice,
for any type of comfort or assurance.

I don't want to waste time searching for
a light at the end of the tunnel
if light breaks 200 miles away.
I can't journey that far on my own.

Right now, I look up and see no ending.
Could You whisper how much farther until paradise?

Stevie Saldivar

Selfishness does not go down without a fight.
It will be dragged away claws scratching and all.
When the battle gets rough, I'll speak to Selfishness-

"You're dying, old friend. And I'm going to watch
you suffocate."

Seasons are each timely and particular,
bringing in anew after purging what no longer can be.

I'm waiting for that rush to come-
the one that sweeps me off of my feet and
leaves me thinking with gratitude,

"It all aligns and makes perfect sense."
Thank you for this season. Thank you for the end.

Stevie Saldivar

When Fear comes knocking with threat in its voice,
convincingly proclaiming that it has you surrounded-

Go boldly within to the Light
that joyfully pronounces us
stronger than Fear.
Be reminded of your sword,
open the door,
look Fear dead in the eyes,

and give him a wink.

Some who thought they would never
taste the poisoned waters of it get served a full cup.

-postpartum

Stevie Saldivar

I've got that tragic look about me
with scars all on my skin.

But You've got You're healing hands around me
and the hope I need to begin.

Maybe it's the way You wash over me like water
in all of your fluidity
taking each previous day off of me-

Maybe it's the knowing
that I can submerge myself in You
and when I'm taken by Your river,
I can finally breathe.

Stevie Saldivar

You aren't going to please everyone in the way
you effortlessly live with no unction
of looking back.
But maybe you're not supposed to.
Your gaze is captured by the glowing, beckoning
horizon-
Be very, very unapologetic about that.

It was easier for me to stay quiet,
but an easy life was no longer appealing to me.

Stevie Saldivar

I will be broken
over and over again
if it means I will be rebuilt softer.

Press down hard on me
until I am gentle,
until I look more like You.

Everywhere we turn
they demand us to consume,
to want,
to feel empty and without.

This is why I long for nature-
for creation that sings to the Heavens
and calls for me to join in nothing
but a melody.

Stevie Saldivar

We don't write to feel.
We write because we refuse
to stop feeling everything.

I was supposed to be the exception.
Broken and battered,
misinformed and misguided,
hateful and cold.

Your hands weren't supposed to welcome me.
Your arms, not able to carry my tired,
confused, stumbling body.

I was supposed to be the exception.
Your mind wasn't supposed to know mine,
Your ears weren't supposed to hear me,
and Your words surely couldn't reach me.

But they did.

You are enough.
Even when I'm blind,
even when I'm silent,
even when my mind considers
You to have exceptions.

Stevie Saldivar

I know one thing for sure
and possibly only this one-
I will have no power over this darkness
until I divorce it.

It is the days that I use
gratefulness as a weapon
that I feel the most alive.
I open my heart and
kiss the sky.

Stevie Saldivar

All of my pieces taken from the floor
are brought back into alignment.
My vision, once blurred, is sharp and quick.
This dead heart has been made entirely new-
and all it took was one look from You.

Maybe the ocean is ferocious
and making it out will take some time,
but you were made to ride this wild wave-

The moon will guide you through the night.
Keep your eyes on the light.
Keep your eyes on the light.

Although I may not be fearless,
I am brave.
Although I may not be unrivaled,
I am passionate.
Although I may not be complete,
I am whole.

When your heart is pounding
and your breath halts
and you can feel the blood moving through your veins,
realize this is your chance-
a chance for change.
Lift your gaze,
demand your own exhale
and make your move.

I bet you'll be able to almost feel
the stardust wash over you.

Stevie Saldivar

Life asks us to dance
and in our victories, we will salsa.
But in our traumas,
the most delicate slow song
will fill the empty space.
It's okay to barely move your tired feet.
Go at your own pace.

The world doesn't stop turning for anyone
even when we think that it should.
When we lose someone we love
that's especially when we wish it would.

Can time halt for one moment only
to bid farewell to Earth's greatest souls?
For the ones who got to see it all
and for those who never got to grow old,
my world stops turning for you.

-Honor

Stevie Saldivar

Though we walk about giving applause to things
that would not exist without You,
You give us eyes.

Hands formed out of pure love and light
will move those pieces in you that no longer fit.
The ones that are broken or bent
and misshaped.
With one touch of warmth and purpose-
there you'll be.
An entirely illuminated, new kind.
It does not matter how long it takes,
those hands will never leave you undone.

Have you ever had a sure thing wither?
A flower awaits Spring only to be pulled up at the
roots-
too quick to cry or howl with any pain.
Justice won't arise until this flower is in
a bouquet choir singing I'm Sorry-
The bloom was never meant for its own vain
satisfaction.
Its sure thing was always destined for someone else.

Strip down my soul-
I'll breathe You in with my
last gasp for air.

Stevie Saldivar

The clenching of my jaw
makes me aware of how tightly
I'm holding on.

I can feel anger in my wrists
and hopelessness in my chest.

But this does not have to be so
when I was made to fight back.

I'll kill what tells me You're not honest,
I'll suffocate the accuser until I feel the release
in my bones.

There was then,
there was you,
and there is now.

-a mark of time.

Stevie Saldivar

I have fallen in love with the hope of it all-
everything could turn for the better.

She met her moment-
the one that draws the line in the sand,
separating then and now.

The lines we don't get to make for ourselves
seem to be drawn harshest.
The moments that are unexpected
throw the hardest punch.

Stevie Saldivar

My womb was home for a tender heartbeat,
a young soul sent for Earth.
I soon realized I was destined to conquer
the battle of letting go.
Our 'see you soon'
was so powerfully disguised as goodbye.

I stopped waiting for my new beginning
and I started demanding it.

Stevie Saldivar

Art is like play-
it's freedom.
It's the wind through your hair.

Nothing quite compares
to never feeling heard
and then all at once
hearing those thoughts spoken
back to you word for word-
the ones you never dared to speak aloud.

"He hears me," she thought,
"and He still loves me."
A twist in the story that will
bring even the most proud
to their knees.

Stevie Saldivar

Sometimes I sit and feel icy wind
to let it build chill bumps all over my legs
because I never know if I'll ever
feel the extremity of this wind again.
My habit of indulging in the thrill of things
has brought me joy but also
cold, cold skin.

I am left here tied in knots
and with longing hands,
grasping for what once was.
Reaching for your laugh or
that look-
those pauses that held so much.

Death is like a volcano
erupting from beneath our feet
covering everything with
lava memories.

This hurts because it's tangible.
This hurts because death was
never meant for us
but we've allowed it in.

Stevie Saldivar

The fall hurts but a bruised knee
only lasts so long.
Those scoffs you may hear
are from those whose pride is placed
too high on a pedestal and are
one small wind from hitting pavement
themselves.

Pay no mind, save your precious time.
Reach for those who have conquered
the battle of getting back up,
no matter the damage that's been done.
They'll sing with you the beautiful tune
of repentance, and remind you that
the battle has already been won.

Rip down the barriers,
release your closed hands,
and give up the key to those
locked parts of your soul.
Human connection,
a listening ear-
sitting in pure silence after
revealing curiosities to another
with no fear.
This is harmony and
this is holy music.

Stevie Saldivar

We are all tourists.
Don't forget that when someone is lost,
or confused,
or not accustomed to your ways.
Don't forget that when someone leaves,
as this has been temporary from the start.
We're all visiting
and we're all searching for home.

You're here and there
and back again-
I'm trying to hold on but
you're older, stronger,
and singing loud.
I hope that it's still my song.

Be honest in your pursuit
and the light will always
guide you home.

I'm learning to not ride these waves of hate,
to not let myself dive so deep into fear.
I used to be so good at being engulfed by
the fire of comparison
but You've taught me that feelings aren't facts.
So, I'll make observations of hindering
emotions and boundaries.
I will no longer lack.
I'm making space for You-
the only reality I need.

Stevie Saldivar

This must be felt and not just heard.
Like the color that fills our lungs at dusk
when it's no longer day but not quite yet night.
Everything is so thick with periwinkle and indigo.
Every tree and dew drop on the grass-
periwinkle and indigo.
Even the stillness in the air is reflecting shades
of this true, pure, almost night-ness.
The atmosphere is so rich and good.
You won't hear me unless you've
felt it.

It's in our very design to be storytellers-
a Storyteller dreamed us up.

Stevie Saldivar

Don't be afraid when you feel
as if you've been buried,
you've been here before-

Look up and grow.
Look up and bloom.

Who told you to be tame
and why did you decide to listen?

Stevie Saldivar

It's been happening since before
time itself-
the beauty in the hymn of the rocks.
You aren't in need of anything,
so that's where I'll rest.
It's just love for the sake of love.

Reach for the light no matter
how far it seems.
No matter if you're almost blind,
no matter if all you can
manage to illuminate
are your fingertips.
That is all you need-
the reach is all you need.

Stevie Saldivar

You have too much power
to be the only one
standing in your way.

Questions will build walls in front of our feet
if we don't ask them.
Shout off the rooftops
from the very depths of your soul
and seek to know no matter the off-putting stares-
that you asked the hard questions
and didn't let your curiosity build animosity but
a candle lit path to guide the way.

Stevie Saldivar

You can chop all of your hair off,
get the tattoo,
you can even dance drunkenly
under the crystal moon.
But when you wake up
and look at the new you
face to face,
you'll realize once again
nothing else can take His place.

I don't know if I'll ever go back
to who I was before it all.
I don't think I would even want to.
I've been challenged and stretched into
a completely new form.
Though I don't recognize myself
in the mirror,
I like the way I look now.

Where there was once doubt
written in my eyes,
I see trust.
The worries that swept
across my forehead
have since been replaced with
flower blossoms of faith.
My once closed hands are
wide, wide open.

I've been through hell
and back again.
But it has prepared me
for what's ahead.
I like the way I look now.

It's alright to know that you must move
but be unsure of how to put
one foot in front of the other.
Lift your eyes to the
women who have gone before you.
They are there to show you
how to chase the light.

Light chasers,
music makers,
full hearted women who
march the skies.
I am you
and you are me-
we're same spirits
and our words fly high.

Stevie Saldivar

Who knows what God will say
to me today or to you today
and at what moment big or minuscule
He will choose to say it.

What I do know is that God is speaking.
Sometimes we hear Him
in the wind or water.
Sometimes we hear Him in the stillness
or silence.

Knowing when He is going to speak
is one of our greatest longings.
Our greatest hope is that we believe,
no matter what,
His voice will reach our hearts.

I'll follow You
over the fences I've built
and to the moon-
walking barefoot into the unknown
and picking daisies from the milky way
with each trusting step.

Stevie Saldivar

If I lean a little to the left on this emotion
and a little to the right on another,
before I know it, I've fallen over.
I'll adjust my posture upright-
to keep my eyes on the glow of the Heavens.
My mind follows and my body aligns
so I don't hit the floor
but instead use my wings to fly.

When nothing satisfies-
not the like or the favorite,
or the opinion or praise,
when everything and everyone
starts to look the same-
instead of becoming bitter when
I'm reminded that the world
is not enough,
I'll jump into the fire
and call this worlds bluff.
I'll look past the surface,
over the walls and
empty things,
and let the Spirit fill my heart
with entirely new dreams.
We can rest easy, sweet sisters,
knowing this was never what it seemed.

-free

Maybe it's not about knowing you'll make it
but knowing you've finally made the decision
to get off the fence and believe
that you're worth it to never quit.

I became shriveled treading shallow waters
for far too long.
I want the depths of it all or nothing.

Stevie Saldivar

Their voices would get tangled in my hair
and no matter what I did,
I couldn't stop their words from marching
into my ears.

Forgive, forgive,
my hearts drum would beat.
But all the louder these words would scream.

I needed an alarming sound
to drown it all out-
something much grander.

Then I lost focus as I felt some-
One take ahold of my hands,
ahold of my mind,
ahold of my thoughts,
as we met eye to eye
and all the noise was gone.

Sometimes letting go is agony
and other times,
a sprint in the opposite direction.
Both take effort and demand
a choice to be made.
If this is true,
then we can count on effort and choice
when we need to welcome the very things
we are too afraid may cause us agony
or tired legs.

Take notice the way you speak to others
and to yourself-
you are either building worlds
or destroying them.

I didn't need impressive words.
I needed power and change.
I needed someone who could
listen without trying to fix me,
who could just remind me of
my real name.

Stevie Saldivar

Gratitude is a superpower
that guides our gaze to thoughtful touches
and beauty that often goes unseen.
Ugly tones ring from complaining,
blocking ear gates from gratitude-
and all it takes is one tiny seed.

Like most beloved acts of life-
healing, relationships, or adventure,
writing to me is very much the same.
You just have to show up, make your
presence known, and let truth
fan your flame.

Stevie Saldivar

I allowed myself to heal
and I made room to grow.
My support was fleeting and
most of them let go.
But nobody batted an eye when
I was passed out in my vomit,
scraping drugs off of the floor.
Maybe it's because I'm not
down there with them anymore.

Comfort has its promises
but I can no longer indulge
in what I'm trying to defeat.

Stevie Saldivar

We have value and purpose,
we are seen and we are heard.
Know this- live this,
to watch your chains be ripped apart
and hear them hit the floor.

Dreaming big is graciously relative.
For some it's a big home to call their own.
For others, a child making home
within a barren womb.
And still, for others, water to quench their thirst
that never ends.

Stevie Saldivar

Victory may not be yelling
from rooftops and dancing
across their chimneys.
Victory may be quiet and
triumphant.
And it can be still-
a steady turning from
and then turning towards
something new.

Those He first appeared to were women-
that must mean something special.
She who was first sent to speak of the glory
was a woman.
God Himself chose to enter humanity
through a woman.
This means more than something special.

Stevie Saldivar

Unweaving, unraveling and unlearning
things I've believed my entire life
to be rocks I could stand on,
or held down against,
or pressed between-
letting the water smooth me over
and soften me so I can
give myself over to the Potter
and be rebuilt on the wheel.

I dove in and started swimming,
first against the current and then
deep into the darkest blues of the sea.
The deeper I went, the freer I became.
Every minute surrounded by water
I was able to let go of more and more
that kept me defeated-
all hate and envy,
jealousy and apathy.
I came up for air and told you of the magnificence,
how brilliant it was in the depths,
and you scolded me for swimming.
You've been floating in the ocean
all your life and never once
have needed to go down there,
you said.
The ocean never asks us to dive, you said.
It doesn't make anybody come alive, you said.

Stevie Saldivar

Navigating through
thoughts and emotions so carefully,
letting myself be and feel.
Trekking over the mountains
and through valleys to overlook
where I know I belong-
the waters of truth.

You can rest here in the uncertainty-
curled up next to your questions,
placing your head gently onto hope,
unsure of what tomorrow will bring.
It's okay to rest here.

Stevie Saldivar

I can sense wide, gaping holes
and lack that is unmeasurable and unable
to be sewn shut.
I am not sad just very aware
that every inch of my soul is craving
to be complete.
I know that these craters must be filled
with more than words or stardust.
They call to something far more
mysterious and glorious than the galaxies-
these parts of me call to some One.

I'm inspired by the dreamers-
those who need to be brought back
down to Earth every so often,
over those too fearful
to look up and wonder what life would be like
if we sat amongst the stars.

Stevie Saldivar

I refuse to demand cruel perfection of myself-
I will always only strive for truth.

Release the pages from your hands,
the photos from the back of your eyes,
your voice from the dreams inside-
Run with grit and purpose.
Run as fast and as far as you can.

Be the encourager.
It is a gift to be able to see into others meant to be's.
It's a power to use your words this way-
letting each one become a sure step for someone
with wobbly knees.
Build, sweet soul, build.

Let us not be so focused on perfect
that we lose sight of sweet surrender.

Stevie Saldivar

We reap what we sow-
be intentional,
don't simply go with the flow.

Just because He may have
came to us as thunder
does not mean He will not
meet with us as warm
morning Light.

Stevie Saldivar

We can lose something or someone
to matters out of our own hands
and still feel hopeful,
all at the same time.
We can experience grief and still, gratitude,
all at the same time.
We are able to be thankful for circumstances
that sometimes cause us great sorrow,
all at the same time.
We are so beautifully complex and
emotions don't emerge from our heart alone-
polar opposites can meet in the middle,
in the soul, and burst with one end of color
as well as the other.
All at the same time.

Doubt bites hard but I bite back.

I was conditioned to only care for tomorrow
but my rebellion is considering eternity.

Sweet, glorious surrender,
dancing upon my worries and regrets,
giving my last breath to say
I know, I trust, I'm here with You.

-praise

Sometimes you won't know what's next.
You won't be able to plan ahead but
this is the waiting- the wilderness,
where you'll learn to howl at the moon,
dance under the stars,
and be patient with yourself until you
feel the calling of the Heavenly bloom.

My eyelids opened letting in light stronger than day
and more warming than summer
and I could feel its rays
illuminate every piece of my soul.
How sweet this is to know with an unveiled face-
the light that makes all things grow.

Why would I change my hue to convey yours
when we can exist as such beautiful
complimentary colors?

Gratitude

To my mom, thank you for your fire and tenacity. You've poured out your life for me and I'm walking to the beat of my drum because you showed me how. I wouldn't be the woman I am without your patience, example and love.

To my dad, thank you for your sacrifice that allowed me to try and fail, and try again. You built a life for me with your own hands and always, always listened with no agenda. Because of you I learned how to do the same for others.

To my brother Josh, the calm and logic to my crazy and emotion. I don't know if there is anyone I hold in such a high esteem as you. Thank you for showing me how to be better.

To my pastors and family, Isaiah and Nino, thank you both for continuously picking me back up when I counted myself out and demonstrating the courage and strength I need to fight the good fight.

Stevie Saldivar

To all my sisters, my safe space- Cherish, Ashley, Alyssa, and Sunshine, thank you for listening and encouraging me to go for life. You all keep this journey fun and I'm thankful to get to walk beside each of you. Thank you for constant inspiration.

To Rachel, Stephani, and Cassandra, my soulmates and friends. Thank you for the 2 am conversations and unconditional love through every season. I don't know what I did to deserve any of you.

To my Grandma and Papa, thank you for always showing up. Knowing I have always been able to count on you both has filled me with love since I was a child and that love blossoms in me still.

To Brittany, Jasmine and Andrew, thank you all for the push. For showing me life is what I make of it and that there truly is no limit in persistence and love.

To Janelle, thank you for your example of a laid down life that I can constantly look towards when I need to be guided to truth and love. Your empathy and conviction mirrors Christ and have imprinted on me forever.

To Nina Valerie, thank you for telling me over and over to write. the. book. For teaching me that God made the good stuff and there isn't anything a good laugh or good prayer can't fix.

To Lillian, thank you for hearing me and letting me cry at your kitchen table. Your welcoming heart healed a part of me I desperately needed to be made new.

To Sarah Turner, my friend and cover artist, thank you for your dedication and time put into this dream.

To my husband, my muse and encourager, thank you for seeing me and jumping with me into the sea of love over and over again. I'll spend forever thanking you for this adventure.

To every person who has ever read anything I've written- thank you for showing me the power of connection and testimony. What a miracle it is that we get to walk this Earth at the same time; thank you for letting me grow with you.

Lastly, my gratitude extends to the One who sees me, hears me, and calls me by name. Thank You for setting me free.

Stevie Saldivar

Made in the USA
Middletown, DE
04 February 2021

33074534R00060